The Feelings Library

by

Asaf Rozanes

THIS BOOK
BELONGS TO

MINDFUL MIA CLUB

Join the *Mindful Mia Club*!

Our amazing members take an active part in the book writing process and are an important part of our worldwide family!

Members also get FREE coloring pages, books and members only promotions.

https://mindful-mia.com/subscribe

*To my Mia
the passion, light and power behind everything I do*

It was another bright, sunshine-filled day in Paradise Valley as Mia woke up. She yawned, stretched, and wiggled her toes.

What a wonderful sleep she'd had. She was so happy she'd checked out "happiness" from the Feelings Library on Tuesday. Now it was Friday, and she was feeling fantastic.

But today, Friday, her feelings were due.

Everyone in Paradise Valley went to the Feelings Library to check out and return their feelings.

Mrs. Brown went after her puppy got sick to check out some sadness.

Mr. Singh went in the other day to check out some anger because his phone bill was too high again.

Katie, from school, checked out some silliness, which was a way for her to be happy.

Mia put on her shoes, grabbed her Feelings Library card, and went outside.

She ran through the grass, free as a bird, so happy and light.

And then she saw her friend, Noah, he was holding himself tightly.

She ran over to him and looked at him and then up at the oak tree he was standing under.

"What's wrong?" she said.

"I'm so afraid," he said.

 "I checked out 'fear' from the Feelings Library because I knew I'd climb this tree if I didn't. I'd go to the top, and then I might fall."

Mia touched his shoulder, but he startled because he was so afraid.

"I think you'd better return your fear today," she said.

"It's okay to be afraid sometimes, but we have to overcome our fears."

"You're right," said Noah, "I'll go with you."

They hurried along, and as they went, they saw someone had trampled the daisies in Mrs. Brown's yard.

"What a shame," said Mia.

Now they saw another friend, Charlotte, who was wiping away tears.

She sat on her step, twirling her pigtails, as little teardrops ran down her cheeks.

"What's wrong, Charlotte?" said Mia.

"I'm so sad," she said. "I checked out sadness from the Feelings Library yesterday because I can't see my grandma this week. I have to wait until next month! I miss her!"

"Come with us," said Noah, as he shivered. "We're... we're... we're going to the..."

"We're going the Feelings Library," said Mia. "Come along, Charlotte, and we'll return your sadness."

And so, off they went, Mia, Noah, and Charlotte.

Along the way, they saw garbage on the road.

"What a shame," Mia said. "Let's pick it up and throw it away." And so, they did.

Soon, they were coming near the Feelings Library when they heard some growling.

They hurried over to the playground, where they saw Henry, who was known as the school bully.

Henry was stomping across the grass, kicking toys and squishing flowers.

"I don't like you!" he said. "And I don't like you! And I really don't like you!"

Mia smiled and said, "Henry, you really should return your anger to the Feelings Library."

But Henry shook his head. "Ha!" he said, smirking. "My anger is two weeks late! And it's not going back anytime soon. I smashed flowers today, threw all my garbage on the ground, and now I'm going to break these toys."

He started to smash a toy truck.

"Come on, everyone," said Mia.

She and the others hurried past Henry, who shouted and swung his fists.

Soon, they made their way to the Feelings Library. It was a building made of beautiful marble with gold lettering.

They climbed the steps as people laughing, crying, and singing poured in and out of the building.

Mia, Noah, and Charlotte made their way to the returns desk.

"I'm... sorry... children, one moment, please." Said Mrs. Jackson the Feelings Librarian.

She swiped her Feelings Library card on the reader and stopped laughing.

"Oh my, that's better," she said. "Being overjoyed is fun, but not forever."

THE FEELINGS LIBRARY

"I'm here to return my happiness!" Mia said brightly.

"And... uh...?" said Noah.

"He's here to return his fear," Mia said.

Charlotte began to cry. "And I need to return my sadness," she sniffed.

One by one, everyone returned their feelings.

THE
FEELINGS
LIBRARY

"You know why it's good to return our feelings to the Feelings Library?" asked Mrs. Jackson.

Mia, who seemed calm now, said, "One type of feeling is too much sometimes."

"Boy, isn't that true," said Noah, wiping the sweat from his brow. "Who would want to be afraid all their life?"

Charlotte's tears were just now drying. "Or sad? It's too overwhelming, Mrs. Jackson. I love having feelings, it's what makes us human, but we have to have a variety."

"It's what makes life so varied and wonderful," said Mrs. Jackson. "I love to laugh, but how could I get my job done if I were laughing all day?"

RE-FEEL
STATION

Suddenly they heard some banging outside. Everyone ran out to see Henry smashing boxes in front of the library.

"I don't like you!" he roared. "Or you either! Hey, get out of my way!"

He smashed more and more boxes and then punched a stop sign.

"Ouch!"

Mrs. Jackson shook her head. "Oh, poor Henry."
"He's a bully," said Noah.

"It's because he never returns his anger to the Feelings Library," said Mrs. Jackson. "Henry, come here, please."

STOP

He stomped over.

"WHAT?" he shouted, his face red.

"Henry, reach into your pocket," said Mia kindly.
"And, Henry," said Noah, "pull out your Feelings Library card."

"Oh, and, Henry," Charlotte added, "return your anger. It's gone on long enough. Let it go."

"But," said Henry, "I… I don't even know why I'm doing this. I can't remember!"

 "Come here, Henry," said Mrs. Jackson. "Hand me your card. If you do, you'll release your anger and return it to the Feelings Library."

ANXIETY
CALM
HAPPINESS
DESPAIR

Henry handed his Feelings Library card to Mrs. Jackson. She pulled out her portable feelings reader, swiped the card, and suddenly, Henry's face returned to normal.

His fists relaxed, his shoulders slumped, and his breathing slowed down.
"Wow," he said, shaking his head. "I thought I needed to keep that anger with me."

"Why'd you hold onto your anger for so long, Henry?" asked Noah. "You could've returned it a long time ago and felt better."

Henry shook his head and wiped his brow. "I don't know," he said. "I can't actually remember. I just couldn't stop being mad."

"Do you see, children?" said Mrs. Jackson. "This is what happens when we hold onto our feelings for too long."

"It takes over everything," said Henry. "And you can't do anything else but feel angry."

"Or happy," Mia said.

Noah nodded. "Or afraid."

"Or sad," Charlotte said.

Together, Mia, Noah, Charlotte, and Henry withdrew some happiness from the Feelings Library, and they went to experience it together at the park.

A note from Mia & Dad

Thank you for purchasing our book and joining us on our *important* mission to *empower children and parents* all over the world!

If you enjoyed reading this book, we would love to read your honest review.

Reviews help us tremendously as they get our books noticed so we can continue our mission to empower more children and parents around the world!

Thank You!

Mia & Dad

Mia and Dad sprinkled and scattered love all over this book!

Were you able to notice and find all the heart shapes we scattered around?

Spoiler Alert:

The next page contains all the hidden locations, flip the page at your own risk ☺

Pssst…Here's where we hid the heart shapes:

<u>Page 7:</u>
Above the bed curtains

<u>Page 11:</u>
Between the boy and the tree trunk

<u>Page 19:</u>
On the big yellow flower

<u>Page 32:</u>
On the wooden bench

<u>Page 34:</u>
On the big stone on the bottom left

Mia and Dad just LOVE to color and we're sure you do too!

So we've added a few of our early book sketches just for you to color in any way you like.

Make the sky pink and the grass blue, it's all up to you!

More books by Asaf Rozanes

Mindful Mia - Award-Winning Children Empowering book series

Short Or Tall Doesn't Matter At All (Mindful Mia, Book #1)

Through an inspiring tale about the sun and the moon and how everyone, no matter how different they are has unique traits and skills, this real life story shows parents and kids alike what is really important in life - like having a good heart and turning bullying into new friendships.

Tomorrow Is Near, But Today Is Here (Mindful Mia, Book #2)

The stress, worry and anxiety our children face is greater than any generation before. I wrote this book to assist my daughter with anxiety and her worries; have a positive perspective on experiencing and enjoying life and what it may bring. Surprisingly this also drastically reduced the time it now takes her to fall asleep.

Part Of The Rainbow (Mindful Mia, Book #3)

In this witty and colorful tale, Mia arrives at the first day of school and is shocked to her green whiskers by what she experiences there and how it would change her life forever!

The Monster Friend (Mindful Mia, Book #4)

Monsters are REAL! It's time to stop ignoring their existence and start to get to know them and why they came to pay us a visit. Join Mia in this inspiring tale about confronting your fears.

The Feelings Library (Mindful Mia, Book #5)

There are no bad feelings, we should learn to experience all our feelings - from happiness to anger - to find what they teach us about the world, about others, about our thoughts but mostly about us.

Even more books by Asaf Rozanes

Fairy Fights

Losing your first tooth can be scary. But Mia and a pair of fairies make it fun! Read Fairy Fights, and soothe your child's fears today!

Staying At Home

This book was written for days like today - Whether you're sick, in quarantine or at home have to stay. A funny and inspiring book to help spend your long times at home in a fun and productive way!